Cromosys Publication

DYNAMIC GRAMMAR of ENGLISH

NIRANJAN JHA SHOWMAN

Founder - Niranjan Jha Showman

cromosys ®
Corporation

Education and Technology Research Center
Patankar Park, Nallasopara (W), Mumbai. +91-9561450045
Education, Technology, Publication, Healthcare, Newsmedia, Realtor, Filmmaking
www.facebook.com/cromosys

+91-9561450045
Learn Advanced Skills
And Get Job Instantly
GERMAN
Python
FRENCH
C++
SPANISH
Java
ENGLISH
HTML5
RUSSIAN
CSS
JavaScript
Cromosys
Education and Technology Research Center
Nallasopara (W), Mumbai

Learn Web Programming

Demo-Class Free

HTML

CSS

React

JavaScript

Typescript

Bootstrap

Cromosys

20 Years of Experience

Nallasopara (W), Mumbai

+91-9561450045

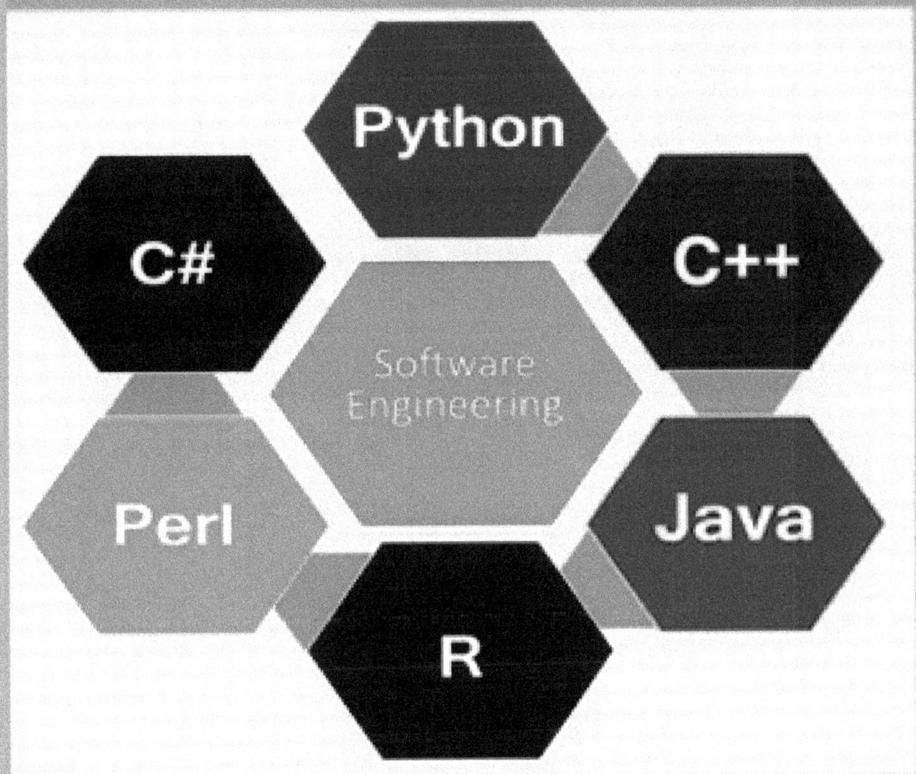
+91-9561450045
Learn Software Engineering
Demo-Class Free
Python
C#
C++
Software
Engineering
Perl
Java
R
Cromosys
20 Years of Experience
Nallasopara (W), Mumbai
+91-9561450045

25 Years of Experience
Learn Visual Multimedia
Animation VFX
Movie Editing
Game Development
Cromosys
+91-9561450045
Education and Technology Research Center
Nallasopara (W), Mumbai
www.facebook.com/cromosys

Jobs Available
For Candidates Who Know

German

French

Spanish

Vacancy in Germany, France, Spain

For Hospitality, Engineering, IT Sector

With Free Visa, Airfare and Accommodation

Cromosys
Education and Technology Research Centre
Nallasopara (W), Mumbai
+91-9561450045
20 Years of Experience

Cromosys Publication

Dynamic Grammar of English

Niranjan Jha Showman

"Education taken with zeal educes to success."
~Niranjan Showman

Preface

Cromosys Publication's **Dynamic Grammar of English** book is an optimal quality guide to the advanced learners of English language. It is an unmatchable unique book of its kind that guarantees your improvement. The lessons and study materials uniquely designed are based on my fifteen years of research in linguistic field. The text, audio and video are magnificently powerful to bring you into linguistic light. Since English is accepted as a global language, the people around the world have been sharpening their knowledge to be good in it. Sometimes, only working knowledge of it doesn't work, and you feel that there is a lot more to explore. The accurate and profound knowledge of this language, which was considered to be existing only in England and America in past, has influenced zillions of mind today, therefore I conceived the idea of making this book a guideline for those who want to be perfect in it.

The significance of this book is that it is dynamic, systemic and blissful with abundance of pure and perfect set of rules that took a decade of time in preparation. One alone, being immaturely suggested, spend ages in reading literature, watching movies and listening to the audio which help them to imitate a little but not learn what in actual sense it is, and their never-ending process of Picasso Adventure collects some scattered information which is unworthy to knowledge enhancement, so the aspirants get lost in wilderness. Whether your intention is to travel abroad or plunge deep into your research, you have to be good in English to survive in today's world. Around eight years ago I went to the USA where I got a chance to get an exclusive training of English. I have been communicating with English-speaking people around the world while managing a team in several call centers, and in part time, I have been teaching this language globally with high exposure. So being able to understand linguistic science, I would like to assure you that the knowledge that you are going to get from this book will definitely sharpen your ability so that you can make your way of success without any hindrance.

Please be aware that this book is not for beginners. If you are looking for a book of basic level, kindly refer to <u>English Speaking and Grammar</u> book authored by me. After you start the lesson of this book, you don't need to worry about anything but just follow each and everything carefully. Don't procrastinate, over-confide or give up. You are going to do the most beautiful thing for yourself, so be bold enough to complete all the lessons. The sentence constructions, which I have explained in this book in the easiest method I could ever find, will need your practice with strong effort.

The world growing with density has brought enormous opportunity to linguistic talents irrespective of their geographical boundaries. If you ask me how, then my answer is that the first and foremost need of the entire creation nearing eight billion people hankering after knowledge and information is reading. And that need of reading is fulfilled by the people who are efficient in writing and editing. Even what we view on technically sophisticated screen these days is also written and edited before. Now you can understand the infinite rapture that a language creates. I strongly believe this book is useful for the people working for communication-based industry, media houses, entertainment world, and obviously for those who love English. This book will stand a milestone for you in your journey. You may have seen some other English books or CDs full of conversations and dialogues which the students purchase by mistake, but they land up in giving up the hope of learning because it tells you what to do but not how and why to do. It doesn't explain but keep on speaking or talking. Just memorizing the words will not take you anywhere. So I have designed this book with proper set of lessons to make you start your adventure sitting at home beginning with real basic. Having been teaching English to global exposure for last thirteen years, I came across the numerous rules of the grammar which are mistakenly ignored by a great majority of non-native users. They don't even believe that these are grammatical rules. And the result gets disgraceful when they accuse Standard English to be outlaw. Cromosys, our language research and education center, saving human efforts from being wasted, is to make you as good as native English users. This path-breaking pioneer training institute for English Speaking, Mass Communication, Foreign Languages, Computer Training, and Academic Tuition, is committed to enlightening human mind with educational endeavors, and we are doing the same for last successful fifteen years. We not only hope but believe that your success is in your hand now, and this book will take you miles ahead in your expectation. We always respect the views and comments of readers, so for any communication with regards to assistance, enquiry or collaboration, we are always there at your reach as it helps us improve our ability.

Niranjan Jha Showman
Trainer, Author Physician, Entrepreneur, Filmmaker, Activist
Founder of Cromosys Corporation
facebook.com/cromosys
+91-9561450045
cromosys@yahoo.com
Nallasopara (W), Mumbai, India

My other books: -
English Word Power
English Voice Accent and Pronunciation
Teach Yourself German
Teach Yourself French
Teach Yourself Spanish
Be millionaire like me
Dynamic Grammar of English
Teach Yourself HTML5
Teach Yourself 3ds Max
Teach Yourself Autodesk Maya
Teach Yourself C Progamming

Cromosys Corporation
Education and Technology Research Center
Education, Technology, Publication, Healthcare, Realtor, Filmmaking
facebook.com/cromosys
+91-9561450045
cromosys@yahoo.com
Nallasopara (W), Mumbai, India

About the Author

Niranjan Jha Showman
Trainer, Author, Physician, Entrepreneur, Filmmaker, Activist

Niranjan Jha Showman is a Language Scientist and Technical Researcher. He is the Award Winning author of more than fifty educational and fictional books at Amazon. He is one of the great-grandsons of the first President of India Dr. Rajendra Prasad. He is a Public Figure, and the globally - renowned Languages Trainer of French, Spanish, and German from past twenty years. Niranjan Jha Showman is an Entrepreneur and also works as a Filmmaker in India. Being the founder and owner of Cromosys Corporation - a company located in Mumbai, India, his company is excelling in the fields of Education, Technology, Publication, Newsmedia, Realtors, Banking, and Cinemascope from past fifteen years.

Niranjan Jha Showman's good-seller educational books and novels are appreciated worldwide. He has more than one million eBook buyers online, and more than one million learners are connected to him globally. One of his novels is critically acclaimed. He is the trainer of French, Spanish, German, English Voice and Accent, and Advanced Computer Education. He is also a political activist in India.

Niranjan Jha Showman is the man who came from rags to riches, he who knows how to turn the table, and he, whom you call the man of Midas-touch. He has observed lives from the Pandora of monkeys to the sanctuary of monks, not only down-to-earth but down-to-grave. He is a B. Com. graduate, and B. Ed. from Delhi University, and diploma holder in French, Spanish and German from America. You can watch his songs, movies, educational videos and many more things by typing "Niranjan Jha Showman" in Google.

Niranjan Jha Showman
+91-9561450045
cromosys@yahoo.com
Mumbai, India
facebook.com/cromosys

Statutory

This book with its content is the registered property of the author Niranjan Jha Showman.
The author and his Cromosys Publication holds all necessary rights of this book.
The copyright certificate of this book is attached at the end of this book.

Lesson 1
<u>Liking</u>

Examples: -
He would prefer dancing to singing.
I would prefer walking to swimming.

*The meaning of the first sentence is that **'He may like dancing more than singing.'** There are many but limited rules of framing the sentences of this kind. They can be framed following any of these rules. Please be careful that any mistake will make the entire sentence incorrect.*

Similar-meaning syntax: -
1. Subject + would prefer + verb^4 + to + verb^4 (Verb^4 = Verb + ing)
   He would prefer dancing to singing.

2. Subject + would prefer + infinitive + rather than + infinitive [without to]
   He would prefer to dance rather than sing.

3. Subject + had better + infinitive [without to] + than + infinitive [without to]
   He had better dance than sing.

4. Subject + had rather + infinitive [without to] + than + infinitive [without to]
   He had rather dance than sing.

5. Subject + would rather + infinitive [without to] + than + infinitive [without to]
   He had sooner dance than sing.

6. Subject + had sooner + infinitive [without to] + than + infinitive [without to]
   He would sooner dance than sing.

7. Subject + would sooner + infinitive [without to] + than + infinitive [without to]
   He would as soon dance as sing.

8. Subject + had as soon + infinitive [without to] + as + infinitive [without to]
   He had as soon dance as sing.

Variation:-
He prefers dancing to singing.
He prefers to dance rather than sing. (Meaning same as above)
He prefers fish to meat.
He prefers Mumbai to Delhi.

Alert: -
Please be careful that after the word <u>prefer</u> 'to' come not than. So don't make sentences like-
~~He prefers dancing than singing.~~
~~He prefers fish than meat.~~
Note: - verb^1 = go, verb^2 = went, verb^3 = gone, verb^4 = going, verb^5 = goes

Lesson 2
<u>Perfect Tense Conditional</u>

Examples: -
We have arrived before the bell rings.
He had reached home before the rain started.
The storm will have come before the rescue operation begins.

The conditional sentences of perfect tense have a fixed rule for their supplementary clauses.

Similar-meaning syntax: -
1. Present perfect clause + before + present indefinite clause.
    She has understood before I tell.

2. Past perfect clause + before + past indefinite clause.
    I had bought the book before you gave me money.

3. Future perfect clause + before + present indefinite clause.
    I will have known the truth before you reveal. (Not, you will reveal)

<u>Correct sentences of this kind</u>: -

We have arrived before the bell rings.
They have deleted the files before we notice.
She had cried many a times before she laughed once.
They had won the battle before they killed any enemies.
The system will have failed before the government realizes.
They will have spread the news before you stop.

Simple Tense Conditional
I will teach her if she requires.
How will you pass the exam if you don't work hard?
She decided to leave after she finished her work.

Alert: -
The Present Perfect and Future Perfect clauses take only Present Indefinite supplementary clauses.
The Future Indefinite (simple) clauses take only Present Indefinite supplementary clauses.
Don't make sentences like-
~~She has understood before I told.~~
~~I will have known the truth before you will reveal.~~
~~I had bought the book before you give me money.~~
~~I will teach her if she will require.~~

Exercise: -
Practice over it by making some sentences for each rule.

Lesson 3
Past Possibility Conditional

Examples: -
She would have purchased a car if you had given money.
If you had given money, she would have purchased a car.
Had you given money, she would have purchased a car.
She would purchase a car if you had given money.

The Past-Possibility Conditional sentences are based on supposition. They have two clauses. The effective part that describes the result (purchasing a car) is called Principal Clause. The Principal Clause always comes with (would have + v³) and the Subordinate Clause is in Past Perfect Tense. Please be clear with these structures as they are very confusing.

Similar-meaning syntax: -
1. Principal Clause [would have + V³] + if + Subordinate Clause [Past Perfect]
   I would have met her if she had come on time. (Long Past – unsuccessful result)

2. If + Subordinate Clause [Past Perfect] + comma + Principal Clause [would have + V³]
   If she had come on time, I would have met her.

3. Had + Subordinate Clause [Past Perfect] + comma + Principal Clause [would have + V³]
   Had she come on time, I would have met her.

4. Subject + would + V¹ + if + Subordinate Clause [Past Perfect]
   I would meet her if she had come on time. (Short Past – less possibility + result still in hope)

Correct sentences of this kind:-

You would have passed the exam if they had taught well.
If they had taught well, you would have passed the exam.
Had they taught well, you would have passed the exam.
You would pass the exam if they had taught well.
Had there been rain, there would have been good crops.
Had you cared for my advice, you wouldn't have regretted.

Alert: -
These sentences have their set-patterns. It needs a lot of practice to learn. Don't get off-track under the influence of your mother-tongue and transliterate them wrongly like this-
~~She had purchased a car if you had given money.~~
~~I think she had purchased a car if you had given money.~~
~~If you had given money, she would purchase a car.~~
~~She would purchase a car if you gave money.~~
~~If you had given money, she could have purchased a car.~~

Exercise: -
Practice over it by making some sentences for each rule.

Lesson 4
<u>Impossible Result</u>

Examples: -
If I were a king, I would make you my queen.
Were I a king, I would make you my queen.
Should I become a king, I would make you my queen.
I wish I were a king, I would make you my queen.

The subject of these sentences always take 'were' as a plural verb not 'was'. They are constructed in past because the results is impossible. Though in speaking 'was' is also used but it is not considered Standard English. In speaking, it goes like – If I was a king.

Similar-meaning syntax: -
1. If + Subordinate Clause [Past Simple] + Principal Clause [Past Simple]
    If I were a bird, I would fly to them.

2. Were + Subordinate Clause [Past Simple] + Principal Clause [Past Simple]
    Were I a bird, I would fly to them.

3. Should + Subordinate Clause [Present Simple] + Principal Clause [Past Simple]
    Should I become a bird, I would fly to them.

4. I wish + Subordinate Clause [Past Simple] + Principal Clause [Past Simple]
    I wish I were a bird, I would fly to them.

<u>Correct sentences of this kind</u>:-

If only I were a bird, I would fly to them.
Would that I were a bird, I would fly to them.
O/Oh that I were a bird, I would fly to them.

If you <u>won</u> a lottery, what <u>would</u> you do? (Past Tense – Result Impossible)
If you <u>win</u> a lottery, what will you do? (Present Tense – Result Possible)

If I bought a car, I would take you for a drive. (Result Impossible)
If I buy a car, I will take you for a drive. (Result Possible)
If I were to buy a car, I would pay in cash. (Result Impossible)
If I have to buy a car, I will pay in cash. (Compulsion)

Alert: -
The sentences of impossible result are always made in past.
If the sky fell, I would catch larks. (Right sentence because sky can never fall)
If the sky falls, I will catch larks. (Wrong sentence because sky can never fall)

Exercise: - Practice over it by making some sentences for each rule.

Lesson 5
Adverbial Emphatic

Examples: -
Some people died, and then <u>came</u> the war.
Whatever I knew, all <u>did</u> I tell the police.
They searched for him, but nowhere <u>was</u> he found.

These Adverbial Emphatic sentences are used to make the statement strong. These are grammatically correct sentences and are being widely used in English. While reading literature, people get confused because they don't understand the meaning.

Syntax: -
Adverb/Conjunction + verb + subject + other words

Correct sentences: -

I play cricket every day.   (Simple sentence)
I do play cricket every day.   (Emphatic, it means – I definitely play every day)
The thief came in.   (Simple sentence)
In came the thief.   (Emphatic – the thief just came in)
He can pass in no case.   (Simple sentence)
In no case can he pass.   (He can't pass at all)

<u>Now see the verities of emphatic which are used only to make the statement strong</u>:-

And next <u>came</u> her sister. ('Came' is placed before 'her' to make it emphatic)
Little <u>did</u> I know about him.
Seldom <u>is</u> he absent.
In no other way <u>can</u> you help me.
Never before <u>did</u> I see such a sight.
Rarely <u>does</u> he study.
No sooner <u>had</u> I started than it began to rain.
Scarcely <u>had</u> the police reached when the thieves fled away.
Hardly <u>could</u> we talk when they locked him inside.
Nowhere was he found.

Just then I saw a tiger.
Only then can you get success.
None else was present there.
And what not did he do?
How else can we fix the problem?
Someone or other was roaming around.
Where else had they left footprints?

Alert – The native speakers use adverbial emphatic in speaking.
And all of sudden he heard a whisper. (Simple sentence)
And all of sudden did he hear a whisper. (Emphatic sentence)

Lesson 6
Choice and Preference

Examples: -
She likes milk.
She has a liking for milk.
She has a weakness for milk.

The sentences of Choice and Preference are framed using various kinds of rules. Learning the varieties of it helps you make beautiful sentences of you own.

Similar-meaning syntax: -
1. Subject + verb [like] + object
   I like this kind of dress.

2. Subject + verb [have] + a liking for + object
   I have a liking for this kind of dress.

3. Subject + verb [have] + a weakness for + object
   I have a weakness for this kind of dress.

4. Subject + verb [have] + a taste for + object
   I have a taste for this kind of dress.

5. Subject + verb [is/am/are] + fond of + object
   I am fond of this kind of dress.

The sentences of similar meaning: -
This dress is to my liking.
This dress is to my taste.
This dress is my choice.
This is my choicest dress.

I don't like it at all.
I have no choice in it.
I just don't like it.
I have an aversion to it.
I am allergic to it.
I can't stand it.
I can't stand this boy.
I can't abide this boy.
I don't approve of this project.

Exercise: - Frame your own sentences and apply them in your composition and speaking.

Note: Present form (V1) = go, Past form (V^2) = went, Past participle (V^3) = gone, Present participle (V^4) (Gerund) = going, V^5 = goes

Lesson 7
<u>Homographic 'Have'</u>

I have a pen. | We have to go now. | Will you have something? | They will have it fixed.

The word 'have' is a very complicating in English. I am listing all the possible meanings of it here.

1. Have = To possess
    I have a computer at my home.

2. Have = To eat or drink
    Will you have a cup of coffee with me?

3. Have = To take
    Have your seat please.

4. Have = To show compulsion
    They have to finish this work today.

5. Have = To get something done
    When will you have your hair colored?

6. Have = To experience
    Her sister had a shock.

7. Have = To instruct or invite
    I will have him call you.

8. Have = To tolerate
    They will not have this insult.

9. Have = To show or feel
    Please have mercy on him!

10. Have = To get
    I had a letter from him.

I have had to teach. *(I have no choice but to teach)*
I have got to teach. *(I have no choice but to teach)*
I had had to teach. *(I had no choice but to teach)*
I am having to teach. (*C*ompulsive continuity)
I could have taught. (I was able to teach but I did not)
I should have taught. (It was my duty to teach but I did not)
I would have taught. (It was possible that I had taught but I did not do)
I may have taught. (Perhaps I have already taught)
I could have had to teach. (I could have taught in compulsive situation but I did not do)
I would have had to teach. (I would have taught in compulsive situation but I did not do)

Lesson 8
<u>Having</u>

Teaching the lesson he shouted at them. | While teaching the lesson he shouted at them. | Having taught the lesson he shouted at them.

The sentence starting with present participle (V⁴) describes that the subject is doing two works, but while doing the first it does the second work also. But, (having + V³+ object) describes that the subject is doing two works, but the second work starts after first work ends.

    Similar-meaning syntax: -
1. Present Participle [V⁴] + subject + verb + other words
   Teaching the lesson he shouted at them.
   (Meaning - He both taught and shouted but he shouted while teaching)
2. While + Present Participle [V⁴] + subject + verb + other words
   While teaching the lesson he shouted at them.
   (The meaning is same as above)
3. Having + Past Participle [V³] + subject + verb + other words
   Having taught the lesson he shouted at them.
   (Meaning - He finished teaching first, then he shouted at them).

<u>**The sentences of similar meaning: -**</u>

Being taught the lesson he shouted at them.
(First part Passive – Someone was teaching him; but after he was taught, he shouted)
Having been taught the lesson he shouted at them.
(The meaning is same as above).
Having been teaching the lesson he shouted at them.
(First part Active – While he was teaching for a long time, he shouted

More examples:-
I remember <u>having to teach</u> them in school. *(I remember teaching them)*
<u>Teaching</u>, I shouted at them. *(I shouted while teaching)*
The sun <u>having risen</u> the fog disappeared. *(After the sun rose)*
The night having come all went home. *(After the night came)*
<u>Opening</u> the box I took out the book. *(I took the book after opening the box)*
<u>Having drunk</u> he fought his neighbors. *(After he got drunk)*
<u>On getting drunk</u> he fought his neighbors. *(After he got drunk)*

Lying in bed I was reading a novel. (Meaning – While lying)
While lying in bed I was reading a novel. (Meaning same as above)
Opening the window he looked around.
Hearing the news he felt very happy.

Lesson 9
Homographic 'Would'

Examples: -
She would meet you next year.
She would meet you last year.
She would come and talk to me for hours.

Though 'would' is the past form of will, but this modal verb has many meanings. Pay attention on the sentences and their meaning written below.

1. Would = Less possibility in future
   She would meet you next year.
   (Meaning – There is a less possibility that she will meet you next year)
2. Would = Less possibility of past
   She would meet you last year.
   (I think [not sure] she met you last year)
3. Would = Irregular habitual action of past
   She would come and talk to me for hours.
   (She irregularly used to come and talk to me)
4. Will is replaced with 'would' in indirect narration
   She told me she would meet me tomorrow.
5. Would = Request
   Would you tell me his address please?

The sentences of similar meaning: -

Will you sing a song, please?
Would you sing a song, please?
Would you mind singing a song?
Would you be so good as to sing a song?

Alert: -
He would learn music last year. (Irregular habitual action of past)
He used to learn music last year. (Regular habitual action of past)
He will learn music. (Simple Future)
He shall learn music. (Strong possibility of future)
He should learn music. (Duty)
He ought to learn music. (Ethic)
He must learn music. (Mandatory)
He is supposed to learn music. (Supposition)

Lesson 10
<u>Wish</u>

I wish I reached on time.
I wish I <u>had</u> reached on time.
If only I reached on time!
If only I <u>had</u> reached on time!

There are two categories of sentences of wishing. In one category, the doer has a strong wish or desire to do the work in present or future. In the other category, the doer's strong wish or desire relates to past because it was unfulfilled.

Syntax (wish to be fulfilled in present of future): -
1. I wish + clause [subject + verb in <u>Past Simple</u>]
   I wish I <u>earned</u> a lot of moncy. ~~(Not, earn or to earn)~~
   (I strongly desire to earn in <u>present</u>)
2. If only + clause [subject + verb in Past Simple]
   If only I earned a lot of money!
   (Meaning same as above)
3. Would that + clause [subject + verb in Past Simple]
   Would that I earned a lot of money!
   (Meaning same as above)
4. O/Oh that + clause [subject + verb in Past Simple]
   O/Oh that I earned a lot of money!
   (Meaning same as above)

<u>The sentences of similar meaning: -</u>
I wish I were a queen.
(I strongly desire to be a queen - in <u>Present</u>)
I wish he were a king.
Would that I were rich.
Would that to be rich!

Syntax (unfulfilled desire of past): -
5. I wish + clause [subject + verb in <u>Past Perfect</u>]
   I wish I had <u>earned</u> a lot of money.
   (I wish I had earned - Unfulfilled desire of <u>Past</u>)
6. If only + clause [subject + verb in Past Perfect]
   If only I had <u>earned</u> a lot of money!
   (Meaning same as above)

<u>The sentences of similar meaning: -</u>
Would that I had <u>earned</u> a lot of money! (Meaning same as above)
O/Oh that I had <u>earned</u> a lot of money! (Meaning same as above)
I wish I had been a queen. (*Thinking in present about unfulfilled desire* of <u>Past</u>)
Would that to have been rich! (*Thinking in present about unfulfilled desire* of <u>Past</u>)
~~I wish I earn a lot of money.~~ (Wrong sentence)

Lesson 11
<u>Comparable</u>

Examples: -
He died.
He is dead.
He breathed his last.

See the list of similar-meaning sentences. It will sharpen your writing and editing skill, and you can add flavors and fragrances to your language.

<u>The sentences of similar meaning:</u> -
He died.
He is dead.
He passed away.
He expired.
He is no more.
He is off. (Slang)
He breathed his last.
It is all over with him.
He gave up the ghost.
He departed from the world.
His soul left for heavenly abode.
He went the way of all flesh.
He paid the debt of nature.

He is angry.
He is in bad temper.
He is out of temper.
He lost his cool.
He is filled with anger.
He got/grew/became angry.
He flew into a rage/temper/fury.
He grew furious.
His eyes flashed fire.
His anger flashed out.
His face flamed still redder.
His face was ablaze with anger.
He was bursting with anger.
He was trembling with anger.
His eyes were full of fire.
He was boiling over with rage.
He was raging and fuming.
He was frowning and growling.

Lesson 12
<u>**Comparable 2**</u>

Examples: -
She is cute.
She is a smasher.
She is exquisitely beautiful.

<u>**The sentences of similar meaning: -**</u>
She is beautiful.
She is cute.
She is a smasher.
She is exquisitely beautiful.
She is a beauty.
She is a dolly.
She is very charming.
She is gorgeous.
She has a sweet face.
She is hot. (Slang)
She is ahem-ahem beautiful.
She looks like an angel.
She has a pleasing personality.
She is a bomb-shell.

She was smiling.
A smile was playing on her lips.
There was a sweet smile on her face.
Her face is wreathed in smile.
She is in ecstasy of joy.
She is in raptures.
She is beside herself with joy.
He joys knows no bounds.
She just laughed.
She burst into laughter.
She laughed up her sleeve.
She broke into a laugh.
She laughed a hearty laugh.
She was roaring with laughter.
She rolled with laughter.

Exercise: -
Write these sentences in your notebook and use them in your speaking.

Lesson 13

Infinite 'To'

Examples: -
I am to teach.
I am to be taught.
I am to have taught.
I am to have been taught.
She looks to have lost.

Infinite To works as a clause or it helps a sentence extend further. To understand a complex sentence or to write a group of sentences giving a Cluster Effect to your text, you need to understand how Infinitive works.

Correct sentences: -
I am to teach him.
(I am about to teach him – Active Voice)
I am to be taught.
(I am about to be taught – Passive Voice)
I am to have taught.
(I am about to have finished teaching – Active Voice)
I am to have been taught.
(I am about to have been taught – Passive Voice)
She looks to have lost.
(It appears that she is lost)
We are sorry to have left you.
(We are sorry as we have left you)

A book had got to be printed. (Had to be – Passive Voice)
A book will have to be bought. (Passive Voice)
I happened to meet him. (Got a chance to)
It is an effort to make people aware. (One time effort)
It is an effort to making people aware. (Continuous effort – Continuous Infinitive)

Alert: -
He was to come. (He was expected to come)
He was to have come. (He was expected to come already before)
They were to teach. (Active Voice)
They were to be taught. (Passive Voice)
Were you to buy this book?
What are they to do now?

Lesson 14

<u>Gerund (V⁴)</u>

Examples:-
He got into the running car.
Running, he got into the car.
Walking is easier than running.
It is easier to walk than run.

Gerund is the Present Participle (V⁴) form of a verb. Being particle, it can be used as a verb or an adjective also.

<u>Correct sentences: -</u>
They are sitting in a garden. (Participle)
Sitting idle is not good. (Gerund)
Sitting, he did all his work. (Participle)

<u>Running</u> is good for health. (Gerund)
We are <u>running</u> in a garden. (Participle)
<u>Running</u>, I threw a stone. (Participle)
They will invest in a <u>running</u> business. (Present Participle Adjective)

She is <u>breaking</u> the windows. (Present Participle)
It is <u>breaking</u> news. (Present Participle Adjective)
This glass is <u>broken</u>. (Past Participle Adjective)

There is a <u>white</u> paper. (Adjective)
This machine has a <u>whitening</u> system in it. (Present Participle Adjective)
Everything is <u>whitened</u> in a second. (Past Participle Adjective)

Gerund and Infinite To

Playing is useful.
To play is useful.
It is useful to play.

Telling lies is a sin.
To tell lies is a sin.
It is a sin to tell lies.
It goes without saying.

Exercise: -
Frame your own sentences using the set of rules of this lesson.

Lesson 15

<u>Though - Although</u>

Examples: -
Though he is rich, he is a miser.
Although he is rich, he is a miser.
He may be rich, but he is a miser.
Rich as he is, he is a miser.

To make compound sentences, you should know the various usages of the conjunctions.

Syntax: -
1. Though + Subordinate clause + comma [not but] + Principal clause
   Though it is costly, it is durable.

2. Although + Subordinate clause + comma [not but] + Principal clause
   Although it is costly, it is durable.

3. Though + Subordinate clause + comma + yet [not but] + Principal clause
   Though it is costly, <u>yet</u> it is durable. (Strong statement)

4. Subject + may be + noun/adjective + but + subject + verb + other words
   It may be costly, but it is durable. (Strong statement)

5. Adjective + as + subject + verb + Principal clause [subject + verb]
   Costly as it is, it is durable.
   However costly it may be, it is durable.

<u>Correct sentences: -</u>

<u>Though</u> you abuse me, I'll continue to love you. (<u>Weak</u> statement)
<u>Even if</u> you abuse me, I'll continue to love you. (<u>Strong</u> statement)
Even though you abuse me, I'll continue to love you. (Strong statement)
No matter you abuse me, I'll continue to love you. (Strong statement)

The sentences of similar meaning: -
I can lend you money if you return soon.
I can lend you money provided you return soon.
I can lend you money provided that you return soon.
I can lend you money on condition that you return soon.
I can lend you money so long as you return soon.

If you do not work hard, you can't be successful. (Don't use, then)
Unless you work hard, you can't be successful. (Strong statement)
They won't move until you reach there. (Unless = condition, until = time)
They won't move till you reach there. (Until and till are same)

Lesson 16

<u>Standby 'It'</u>

Examples: -
To smoke is harmful.
Smoking is harmful.
It is harmful to smoke.

In this lesson, you will learn framing sentences using it, infinitive to, and gerund.

Syntax: -
1. Subject [Infinitive to + verb] + is/was + adjective/noun
2. Subject [Gerund – V^4] + is/was + adjective/noun
3. It + is/was + adjective + infinitive
4. It + is/was + noun + infinitive

Correct sentences: -
To smoke is harmful.
Smoking is harmful.
It is harmful to smoke.
It is a crime to smoke at a public place.
To tell lies is a sin.
Telling lies is a sin.
It is a sin to tell lies.
It is no use to cry.

It seems that they are gone.
It appears that they are gone.
It is said that they are gone.

It is hoped they would go.
It is surprising if they would go.
It is likely to happen.
It is possible to happen.
It is regretted.
It goes without saying.
It is Monday today.

Using 'it' as a subject before infinitive is also Standard English. Infinitive and gerund can also work as a subject in compound sentences.

Alert: -
This is a book. It is new. (An object can be referred first 'this' then 'it')
It is this book not that.
~~Where she lives this is not known.~~ (Don't use of this)

Lesson 17

<u>**WH Words**</u>

Examples: -
How to translate is an art.
How to translate is easy.
What to do is a problem.

Learn to use WH words as connectors in a sentence.

Syntax: -
1.   Phrase [question word + to + verb] + is/was + noun/adjective

Correct sentences: -
How to translate is an art.
How to translate is easy.
What to do is a problem.
What not to do is uncertain.
When to start is undecided.
Where to go is under consideration.
Where she lives is not known.
Why she is sad is a mystery.
That he is poor is known to all.
When he will return is uncertain.

A boy who tells lies gets punishment.
Boys who tell lies get punishment.
One who tells lies gets punishment.
Those who tell lies get punishment.

Syntax: -
1.   Noun + who/that + verb [adjective clause] + verb + other words
2.   One/those + who/that + [adjective clause] + verb + other words

<u>**Correct sentences: -**</u>
A man who works hard gets reward.
I know what you want to say.
She reached where she had to.
It is hard to explain how it works.

The book that is here is mine.
The books <u>that are</u> here are mine. (Not, those are)

Exercise: -
Frame your own sentences using the rules of this lesson.

Lesson 18

<u>Modals</u>

Examples: -
You have to sing.
You had to sing.
You have had to sing.
You had had to sing.

Modals or Modal Verbs are the words that express the mood of a verb in a sentence. There are many Modals that are used in International English. Here you get a unique list of almost all of them.

Correct sentences: -
You have to sing. *(Present Compulsion)*
You had to sing. *(Past Compulsion)*

You will have to sing. *(Future Compulsion)*
You would have to sing. *(Past Possibility + Compulsion)*
You may have to sing. *(Present Possibility + Compulsion)*
You should have to sing. *(Obligatory Compulsion)*
You must have to sing. *(Strong Compulsion)*

You have had to sing. *(You have got to sing).*
You had had to sing. *(You had got to sing).*
You are having to sing. *(You are singing in compulsive situation).*

You have sung. *(Present Perfect Tense)*
You had sung. *(Past Perfect Tense)*
You will have sung. *(Future Perfect Tense)*

You could have sung. *(Past Capacity + Work not done)*
You should have sung. *(Past Obligation + Work not done)*
You would have sung. *(Past Possibility + Work not done)*
You may have sung. *(Past Possibility + Work done)*
You must have sung. *(Present Perfect + Work done)*

You could have had to sing. *(Past Capacity + Compulsion + Work not done)*
You would have had to sing. *(Past Possibility + Compulsion + Work not done)*
You may have had to sing. *(Past Possibility + Compulsion + Work done)*

To remember: -
<u>The Elements of Grammar</u>
Tense, Parts of Speech, Syntax, Narration, Punctuation, Phonology, Etymology, Semantics, Figure of Speech

Lesson 19

<u>**Narration**</u>

*This lesson explains the unique rule of Direct-Indirect Narration that cannot be found anywhere else. *P stands for Person (First Person, Second Person, and Third Person). *R.V. = Reporting Verb, *R.S. = Reported Speech.*

<u>**R V – Past**</u>		<u>**R S – Present**</u>	<u>**Result**</u>
Sayer	**Listener**	**Reported Point**	
1 P	+3 P	+1 P	= 1 P + Past Tense I said to him, "I play." I told him that **I** played.
1 P	+2 P	+1 P	= 1 P + Past Tense I said to you, "I play." I told you that **I** played.
1 P	+2 P	+2 P	= 2 P + Past Tense I said to you, "You play." I told you that **you** played.
1 P	+3 P	+2 P	= 3 P + Past Tense I said to him, "You play." I told him that **he** played.
1 P	+2 P	+3 P	= 3 P + Past Tense I said to you, "He plays." I told you that **he** played.
1 P	+3 P	+3 P	= 3 P + Past Tense I said to him, "He plays." I told him that **he** played.
2 P	+3 P	+1P	= 2 P + Past Tense You said to him, "I play." You told him that **you** played.
2 P	+1 P	+1 P	= 2 P + Past Tense You said to me, "I play." You told me that **you** played.
2 P	+1 P	+2 P	= 1 P + Past Tense You said to me, "You play." You told me that **I** played.
2 P	+3 P	+2 P	= 3 P + Past Tense You said to him, "You play." You told him that **he** played.
2 P	+1 P	+3 P	= 3 P + Past Tense You said to me, "He plays." You told me that **he** played.
2 P	+3 P	+3 P	= 3 P + Past Tense You said to him, "He plays."

			You told him that **he** played.
3 P	+1 P	+1 P	= 3 P + Past Tense
			He said to me, "I play."
			He told me that **he** played.
3 P	+2 P	+1 P	= 3 P + Past Tense
			He said to you, "I play."
			He told you that **he** played.
3 P	+2 P	+2 P	= 2 P + Past Tense
			He said to you, "You play."
			He told you that **you** played.
3 P	+1 P	+2 P	= 1 P + Past Tense
			He said to me, "You play."
			He told me that **I** played.
3 P	+1 P	+3 P	= 3 P + Past Tense
			He said to me, "He plays."
			He told me that **he** played.
3 P	+2 P	+3 P	= 3 P + Past Tense
			He said to you, "He plays."
			He told you that **he** played.

This is the basic rule of constructing sentences in indirect form. To get more knowledge of Narration, you can refer to any High School Grammar book.

D: I said to him, "Do you speak English?"
I: I asked him if he spoke English.

D: He said to me, "How is your friend?"
I: He asked me how my friend was.

D: I said to him, "I played Cricket."
I: I told him that I had played Cricket.

D: The teacher said to the boy, "Will you go home now?"
I: The teacher asked the boy if he would go home then.

D: The boy said to me, "I can read this book."
I: The boy told me that he could read that book.

D: She said to me, "Give me a glass of water."
I: She asked me to give her a glass of water.

D: I said to her, "Don't touch the box."
I: I forbade her to touch the box.

D: I said to him, "Happy holiday!"
I: I wished him a happy holiday.

Lesson 20

<u>**Tense**</u>

Examples: -
He has gone.
He is gone.
He has been absent.
He has been ill since morning.

Please be careful that – come, go, rise, fall, melt, lose are the verbs that directly takes past participle (V^3).

Correct sentences: -
They have gone. (Long time ago)
They are gone. (Short time ago)
She has come. (Long time ago)
She is come. (Short time ago)

<u>**Complex Perfect**</u>
He has been a leader. *(1. He is still a leader. 2. He was but now he isn't)*
He has become a leader. *(Now he has become)*
He has been a leader for ten years. *(He is still a leader)*
He had been a leader. *(He was)*

Active Passive
I am to teach him. (Active)
He is to be taught by me. (Passive)
I was to teach him. (Active)
He was to be taught by me. (Passive)
I have to teach him. (Active)
He has to/has got to be taught by me. (Passive)
I had to teach him. (Active)
He had to/had got to be taught by me. (Passive)
I will have to teach him. (Active)
He will have to be taught by me. (Passive)
I could have taught him. (Active)
He could have been taught by me. (Passive)

To remember: -
<u>The Original Sense</u>

I have to play. *(I have the work to play)*
I have played. *(I have something played)*
I will play. *(I will (will = wish) to play)*

Lesson 21

<u>**Causative Verbs**</u>

Examples: -
He made me sing.
I made him speak.
The boys were made to cry.

The meaning of causative sentences is that the work is got to be done by someone.

Syntax: -
1. Subject + make + noun/pronoun + infinitive [without to]
   I made him laugh. (Not, to)
2. Subject + is/are/was/were + made + infinitive
   She was made to sing.
3. Subject + will be + made + infinitive
   He will be made to speak.

   Horses are made to walk.
   I was made <u>to</u> sing. (Passive Voice – To)

More correct sentences: -
The boss had a letter written. (Not, write)
The boss got a letter written.
She has her hair colored.

I can't get him to understand me.
He can't get her to talk to him.
I got the old watch to work.
She got me to wear a new suit.
I didn't get anyone to do the work.

The boss can have/get a letter written.
The boss could have/get a letter written.
The boss could have/could have got a letter written.
The rich can have/get all this done.

You should get the work done.
You should have the work done.
You should have got the work done.

Alert: -
I could have a letter written. (Causative)
I could have written a letter. (Active)

Lesson 22

<u>Homograph</u>
<u>Get</u>
How much did you get for it? (To achieve)
I am getting cold. (To feel)
She got your point clearly. (To understand)
Get me your manager on the phone. (To avail)
They will get this work done today. (To get a work done)
It is getting darker now. (To happen)

<u>Go</u>
When is he going from here? (To proceed)
Why are you going mad about it? (To become)
How are the mangoes going these days? (To be sold)
This is a big go of my life. (Success)
If you are go, life is good to you. (Progressive)

<u>Look</u>
Look at the girls dancing in the party. (To see)
You look very tired today. (To appear)
Go for the originality, not for look. (Fashion)
The look of this hotel has to be changed. (Appearance)
She gave me a look from the corner. (The direction of eyes)

<u>Do</u>
When are you doing your homework? (To do)
I did English in my school. (To study)
He did the puzzle in a second. (To solve)
It will not do for me. (To be suitable)
I do know him very well. (To emphasize)

<u>May</u>
She may pass this exam. (Possibility)
You may leave now. (Order)
May I have your address please? (Request)
May you get the victory! (Wish)
They <u>might</u> accept my proposal. (Very less possibility)
Truth disappears in the shadow of <u>might</u>. (Power)

Variations:-
If I am to go, I will get all done.
If I get to go, I will get all done.
If I have to go, I will get all done.
If I happen to go, I will get all done.
If it so happens that I go, I will get all done.
If I seem to go, I will get all done. (Colloquial)

Lesson 23

<u>Homograph</u>

<u>Make</u>
Are you making your breakfast? (To prepare)
What business are they making money from? (To earn money)
You have to make it fast. (To do)
Don't make me tell him the truth. (To compel)
Two and two makes four. (To set)

<u>Keep</u>
I kept my books there. (Put)
Do you keep pens? (To have something for sale)
You can't keep me informing the police. (To hold from doing)
What kept you there so long?
He is not keeping well today. (To maintain)
How many keeps does he have? (Illegal wife)

<u>Happen</u>
What is happening there? (To occur)
What should I ask him if I happen to meet? (To get chance)
Happen, he may be late. (Perhaps)

<u>Fall</u>
The ball fell from the top floor. (To descend)
The government will fall. (To lose power)
His eyes fell on me. (To take a particular direction)
It fell to me to answer. (Come by chance)
They will start the business from the next fall. (Autumn)

<u>Take</u>
He took it from me. (To acquire)
Who is going to take this medicine? (To consume)
It will take time. (To use up)
I take your point seriously. (To understand)
He did not take the school assembly. (To conduct)

Note: The usage of <u>Double Negative</u>, <u>Adverbial Emphatic</u>, <u>Litotes Effect</u>, and <u>Idioms and Phrases</u> that I have explained in my book 'English Voice Accent and Pronunciation' will help you sharpen your English more.

Exercise: -
Make your own sentences using these homographs. It will help you to be versatile in your composition, editing and communication skill.

Lesson 24

<u>Introductory 'It' and 'There'</u>
Learn the correct usage of grammar from these examples:-

Introductory 'It'
It is raining. (Introductory 'It')
~~It has stopped raining~~. (Wrong sentence)
Rain has stopped. (Right sentence – 'it' is used at the happening only, not stopping)
It is just on seven. (Meaning: Going to be seven o'clock)
It is getting on for midnight.
It goes without saying.
It is ten to seven. (Meaning: Ten minutes before seven)
~~It is six to seven~~. (Wrong sentence, 'to' is used only with those numbers which are multipliable to '5')
It is sex minutes to seven. ('Minute' is used for those which are not 5x multipliable)
It is quarter after seven. (American usage)
It is quarter of seven. (American usage)

More correct examples:-
Do you know how to tell time?
Do you know telling time?
Do you know how to read the watch?
This watch loses five minutes a day.
This watch gains five minutes a day.
This watch neither gains nor loses.
What time do you make it? (What is your guess?)
What do you make the time? (Meaning same as above)

Introductory 'There'
There is a temple in my village.
There is a cow over there.
There is a tank here.
There lived a saint in my village.
There is a meeting tomorrow.
There are boys in the filed.
The boys are there in the filed. (Emphasis on boys)
There is a boy in the house.
~~There~~ is Steve in the house. (Wrong sentence – 'there' doesn't come with definite noun/pronoun)
Steve is in the house. (Write sentence)
There is here a chair to sit on. (Emphasis on here)
There are more women than men here.

More correct examples:-
What about going there?
How about going there?
Suppose we go there?
Supposing we go there?

Lesson 25
Learn the correct usage of grammar from these examples:-

<u>Conjunction</u>
A boy who tells lies gets punishment.
Boys who tell lies get punishment.
One who tells lies gets punishment.
Those who tell lies get punishment.

No sooner <u>did</u> she reach than the kids fled away. (No sooner/hardly/scarcely takes helping verb next)
Hardly <u>had</u> I started when it began to rain. (Helping verb comes just next)
~~No sooner he went to bed it started raining~~. (Wrong sentence - ~~he went~~, it should be 'did he go')
No sooner did he go to bed it started raining. (Write sentence)
I will call you when you reach there. (Meaning: The moment you reach)
I will call you when you have reached there. (Meaning: After you have reached)
I will call you after you reach there. (Meaning: After sometime)

He walks as if/as though he <u>were</u> lame. (Don't use 'was')
You memorize as if/as though you <u>were</u> a parrot. (Don't use 'was')
It seems as if/as though it <u>would</u> rain. (Not 'will')
I feel like kissing your pen.
However poor he may be, he is happy.
Speak as he will, I won't reply. (Meaning – Let him speak as much he wants)
Speak what he will, I won't reply. (Meaning – Let him speak anything he wants)
Whatever he may speak, I won't reply. (Meaning same as above)

Come what may, I can't change it. (Meaning – Let anything happen)
Whatever may happen, I can't change it. (Meaning same as above)
While he oppresses the poor, I help them.
Whereas he oppresses the poor, I help them. (Meaning same as above)
While on the one had he oppresses the poor, I help them. (Meaning same as above)
In spite of sons, he is helpless.
For all his sons he is helpless. (Meaning same as above)

Variations:-
You alone can't do it.
You yourself can't do it.
You singly can't do it.
You can't do it yourself.

Lesson 26
Learn the correct usage of grammar from these examples:-

<u>**Preposition**</u>
I met him in the morning.
I'll meet him on Monday morning. (Not 'in' – in/at is not used before this/next/last time-indicator)
I will meet him on the morning of first June (Not 'in')
Is there anything on tomorrow? (On = scheduled)
Have you anything on this evening? (On = scheduled)

More examples to learn correct preposition:-
He died <u>of</u> cholera.
He is sick <u>with</u> fever.
He danced <u>for</u> joy.
I am glad <u>of</u> your success.
He is suffering <u>from</u> fever.
He is silent <u>with</u> shame.
She is dying <u>with</u> hunger.
I am fed up <u>with</u> him.
He is shivering <u>with</u> cold.
His face is wet <u>with</u> tears.
His face is red <u>with</u> anger.

<u>**Helping verbs**</u>
The rich are happy.
The sick are helpless.
What to do is a problem.
What not to do is uncertain.
When to start is undecided.
Where to go is under consideration.
Where she lives is not known.
Why she is sad is a mystery.
That he is poor is known to all.
There are two books to read.
Can he tell lies?
Do you think he will tell lies?
Is he likely to tell lies?

I made him laugh.
He is made to laugh.
The boy was made to laugh.
I can't get him understand me.
I got the old watch to work.
He can have a letter written.
He could have had (got) a letter written.
He should have had (got) a letter written.
He would have had (got) a letter written.

Lesson 27
This list of sentences is to make you familiar with correct usage of grammar:-

<u>Comparison</u>
This book is by far the best.
This book is much the best.
This book is the very best.
This book is far and away the best.
This book is far better than that.
This book is better by far.
This book is still better.
This book is better still.
This book is preferable to that.
His pen is better than mine but yours is still better.
Your brother is less tall than you. (Not, taller)
Your brother is not as/so tall as you.
Monica is the taller of the two girls. (Not, than)

Rita is better than any/all other women. (Not, ~~all women~~)
Rita is better than anyone/anybody else. (Not, ~~anybody.~~)
Rita is the best of all women.
A woman can't be better than she. (Not, ~~her~~)
No woman can be better than she. (Not, ~~her~~)
You can't find the like of her.
She is one of the best women if not the best.
This is the best book I have ever written. (Not, ~~that, which~~)

Walking is easier than running.
It is easier to walk than run. (Meaning same as above)
This box is three times as heavy as that box.
~~This box is three times heavier than that box.~~
This box is three kilos heavier than that. (Heavier is used with fix amount)
This shirt is several times as good as that.
~~This shirt is several times better than that.~~
This shirt is five dollars dearer than that.
I want a basketful of mangoes. (Not, a basket of)
He wants a spoonful of sugar.
This room is ten feet by eight feet.
This room measures ten feet by eight feet.
Do you mind my asking you something? (Meaning – Can I ask you?)
Five years have passed since he began the work.
This is the same tea I bought yesterday.
This is the same tea as I bought yesterday. (Similarity in tea)
This is the same tea that I bought yesterday. (Exactly same tea)
The higher we go, the colder it is.
The sooner you begin, the better it is.
The more you get, the more you want.

Lesson 28
This list of sentences is to make you familiar with correct usage of grammar:-

Possession
She has a daughter.
She has got a daughter. (Meaning same as above)
We have no car.
We haven't any car. (Meaning same as above)
We haven't got any car. (Meaning same as above)
We don't have any car. (Meaning same as above)

How much is this pen?
What does this pen cost? (Meaning same as above)
What price is this pen? (Meaning same as above)
How much does this pen cost? (Meaning same as above)
It is five dollars.
It costs five dollars.
How far is it to the bus stop? (Meaning – How far the bus stop is from here?)

Hope and Wish
It is hoped that they will return.
It seems they will return.
It appears they will return.
It is surprising if they return.
It is said they will return.
Their return is likely to happen.
It is possible that they will return.
It is regretted that they have returned.

He had better consult a doctor. (Advice)
He had rather consult a doctor. (Meaning same as above)
He would rather consult a doctor (Meaning same as above)

He needn't beg.
He does not need to beg.
He has not to beg.
He has not got to beg.
He does not have to beg.

God give you success!
May you be successful!
I wish you success.

I may be allowed to go there. (Meaning – I should be allowed – A request)
I may be permitted to go there. (Meaning same as above)
I may be given permission to go there. (Meaning same as above)
Ten to one that she will pass the exam. (Meaning – She will definitely pass)

Lesson 29
The correct usage of grammar:-

<u>Adjective</u>
She lost her only child.
She lost her child only.
Only she lost her child.

Martin is ten. (Age)
Martin is ten <u>years</u> old. (Years, not year)
Martin is a ten-<u>year</u> old boy. (Year, not years)

This house is ten years old.
This is a ten-year old house. (After hyphen, singular noun is used)
~~This house is ten~~. (Wrong sentence – not applicable for non-living thing)
She is getting on for twenty. (Meaning – Going to be twenty)
He is in his teens.
They are in their thirties.
She would be about twenty.

I love you more than him. (Meaning – I and he both love you)
I love you more than he. (Meaning – I love both you and him)

<u>Pronoun</u>
This is a book of William.
This is a book of William's. (One of many)
He is a brother of mine. (One of many)

He is to see me tomorrow. (Meaning – He should meet)
He shall see me tomorrow. (Meaning same as above)
Let him see me tomorrow. (Meaning same as above)

Can I use your phone?
Could I use your phone? (Meaning same as above)
Might I use your phone? (Meaning same as above)
Shall I use your phone? (Meaning same as above)

It may/might rain today. (Might = Less possibility)
Perhaps it will rain today.
Probably it will rain today. (Meaning same as above)
It is possible that it will rain today. (Meaning same as above)
Rain is likely today. (Meaning same as above)
There is likelihood of rain today. (Meaning same as above)
It is going to rain today. (Meaning same as above)
Ten to one that it will rain today. (Surety)
It can't rain today. (Can't = Impossible)

Lesson 30

<u>Article</u>
I am going to school. (Meaning – Same school that I go everyday)
I am going to <u>the</u> school. (To another school)
He lives in <u>the</u> USA. (The is used with United words)
I live in India. (Don't use 'the')

We came <u>an</u> hour ago. ('An' because next words start with a vowel sound)
They are in <u>a</u> university. ('A' because next word start with a consonant sound)
She is <u>an</u> M.A.
He is <u>a</u> Ph. D.
I wished him <u>a</u> Happy Christmas.

I intend to buy <u>a</u> car. ('A' is used with singular countable noun)
I intend buying a car. (Meaning same as above)
My intention is to buy a car. (Meaning same as above)
We must speak <u>the</u> truth. ('The' definite article to specify)
We ought to speak the truth. (Meaning same as above)
We ought to have spoken the truth.

<u>Emphatic Do</u>
Do write in pencil. (Must write)
He does come here everyday. (Definitely comes)
Have a cup of tea, won't you?
Please do have a cup of tea.
Come here, you.
Why not start today? (Don't use 'to start')
Why worry about him? (Don't use 'to worry')

May I go out?
Can I go out? (Meaning same as above)
Could I go out? (Meaning same as above)
Might I go out? (Meaning same as above)

<u>Negation</u>
No smoking here.
You can't smoke here.
You must not smoke here.
You shall not smoke here.
I can't have you smoking here.

Do you mind my smoking here?
Do you mind if I smoke here?
Would you mind if I smoked here?

Lesson 31

<u>State</u>
I am curious to know.
He is anxious to hear.
They are eager to learn.

He cannot change his habit.
He is not able to change his habit. (Meaning same as above)
He is unable to change his habit. (Meaning same as above)
He won't be able to change his habit. (Meaning same as above)

I need hardly mention. (Meaning – I don't need to mention)
I need scarcely mention. (Meaning same as above)
I needn't mention. (Meaning same as above)

She keeps on crying.
She is always crying. (Meaning same as above)
She is constantly crying. (Meaning same as above)

He has the habit of begging.
He is in the habit of begging.
He is used to begging.
He is accustomed to begging.

She is longing for wealth.
She is pining for wealth. (Meaning same as above)
She is hankering after wealth. (Meaning same as above)

Suppose you <u>won</u> a lottery, what <u>would</u> you do? (Winning impossible – because both clauses in past)
Supposing you <u>won</u> a lottery, what <u>would</u> you do? (Winning impossible – because both clauses in past)
Suppose you <u>win</u> a lottery, what <u>will</u> you do? (Winning possible – both clauses in present/future)
Supposing you <u>win</u> a lottery, what <u>will</u> you do? (Winning possible – both clauses in present/future)

He is so rich that he can buy a car.
So rich is he that he can buy a car. (Meaning same as above)
He is rich enough to buy a car. (Meaning same as above)

He is ill so he can't come.
It is because he is ill so he can't come. (Emphatic – Meaning same as above)
As he is ill, he can't come. (Meaning same as above)
Since he is ill, he can't come. (Meaning same as above)
Seeing that he is ill, he can't come. (Meaning same as above)
Now that he is ill, he can't come. (Meaning same as above)

Lesson 32

Present Participle

Examples: -
Lying in the bed I was reading a novel.
Sitting in the tree he was cutting off a branch.

Present Participle is the V^4 continuous form of a verb. Though you are familiar with the examples given in the previous lessons, but here I am explaining it more clearly.

Syntax: -
1. Present Participle + subject + verb + other words
   Walking in a garden I was talking to him.
2. While + Present Participle + subject + verb + other words
   While operating a computer I was listening to the song.
3. Having + Past Participle + subject + verb + other words
   Having typed the letter he posted it.
4. Subject + having + past participle + subject + verb
   The night having come all went home.

Request
Close the gate, please.
Close the gate, will you? (Meaning same as above)
Close the gate, won't you? (Meaning same as above)
Will you close the gate, please?
Would you close the gate, please? (Meaning same as above)
Would you mind closing the gate? (Meaning same as above)

Have a cup of tea, won't you?
Please do have a cup of coffee.

Advice
You might try again. (Advice in present)
Do take complete rest. (Emphatic)
You must consult a doctor.
You had better see a doctor.
Let there be no noise.
Let him begin the work, will you?

Variation:-
It is cold today.
It is too cold today.
It is not hot but rather cold today. (Rather = dislike)

Lesson 33

Ownership
1. Has + subject + noun
Has he a car?
2. Has + subject + got + noun
Has he got a car? (Meaning same)
3. Does + subject + have + noun
Does he have a car? (Meaning same)

More correct examples:-
He is your friend. (Simple possessive)
He is one of your friends. (Simple possessive)
He is a friend of yours. (Emphatic possessive, Meaning – one of many)
This is a pen of mine.
She is a friend of hers. (Not, her)

Command
1. Do + verb
Do see me tomorrow. (Emphatic order)
2. Verb + object + comma + subject
See me tomorrow, you. (Strong command)
3. Subject + is/are/shall + infinitive
You are to see me tomorrow. (Command)
You shall see me tomorrow. (Command)
4. Let + him/her/them + infinitive [without to]
Let him see me tomorrow. (Command)
5. Let + there be + noun
Let there be peace. (Command)
6. Let + subject + be + noun
Let it be a circle. (Assumption)

Prohibition
1. Don't + infinitive [without to]
Don't park here.
2. No + V^4 (ing)
No parking here.
3. Subject + can't + infinitive [without to]
You can't park here.
4. Subject + mustn't infinitive [without to]
You mustn't park here.
5. Subject + shall + not + infinitive [without to]
You shall not park here.
6. Subject + can't have + object + V^4 (ing)
I can't have you parking here.

Lesson 34

Request (Similar sentences)
1. Infinitive [without to] + comma + please
Help me, please.
2. Infinitive [without to] + comma + will you?
Help me, won't you?
3. Just + infinitive [without to] + comma + will you?
Just help me, won't you?
4. Please + do + infinitive [without to]
Please do help me. (Emphatic)
5. Will + you + infinitive [without to] + please
Will you help me, please?
6. Would + you + infinitive [without to] + please
Would you help me, please?
7. Would + you mind + V^4 (ing)
Would you mind helping me?
8. Would + you be so good/kind + as + infinitive [with to]
Would you be so good as to help me?
Would you be so kind as to help me?

Proposal (Similar sentences)
1. What about + V^4 (ing)
What about going to a picture? (Meaning – What is the opinion about going?)
2. How about + V^4 (ing)
How about going to a picture? (Meaning same as above)
3. Suppose + subject + V^1
Suppose we go to a picture? (Meaning same as above)
4. Supposing + subject + V^1
Supposing we go to a picture? (Meaning same as above)

1. It is + no use/no good + V^4 (ing)
It is no use/no good going now.

Variation:-
Shall I talk to you?
Can I talk to you? (Meaning same as above)
May I talk to you? (Meaning same as above)
Could I talk to you? (Meaning same as above)
Might I talk to you? (Meaning same as above)
Shall we talk? (Meaning same as above)

Lesson 35

Permission (Similar sentences)
1. May I + infinitive [without to]
May I come in? (Formal)
2. Can I + infinitive [without to]
Can I come in? (Accepted in speaking)
3. Could/might I + infinitive [without to]
Could/might I come in? (Very polite)
4. Would you mind my + V^4 (ing)
Would you mind my coming in? (Meaning same as above)
5. Do you mind if I + V^1
Do you mind if I come in? (Meaning same as above)
6. Would you mind if I + V^2
Would you mind if I came in? (Meaning same as above)

1. Subject + may be allowed/permitted + infinite [with to]
I may be allowed/permitted to travel by plane. (Meaning – Seeking permission)
2. Subject + may be given permission + infinite [with to]
I may be given permission to travel by plane. (Meaning same as above)

Obligation (Similar sentences)
1. Subject + needn't + infinitive [without to]
I needn't mention.
2. Subject + haven't / hasn't + infinitive [with to]
I haven't to mention. (Meaning same as above)
3. Subject + haven't / hasn't + got + infinitive [with to]
I haven't got to mention. (Meaning same as above)
4. Subject + don't / doesn't + have + infinitive [with to]
I don't have to mention. (Meaning same as above)
5. Subject + don't / doesn't + need + infinitive [with to]
I don't need to mention. (Meaning same as above)
6. Subject + need hardly + infinitive [without to]
I need hardly mention. (Meaning same as above)
7. Subject + need scarcely + infinitive [without to]
I need scarcely mention. (Meaning same as above)

I have some money to spend.
I have some money for spending. (Meaning same)
He has gone to play.
He is gone to play. (Meaning same)

Lesson 36

Double object without 'for'
He got me a pen. (Meaning – He got a pen for me)
She made me a sweater.
I chose him a nice present.
Can you spare me some time?
Will you do me a favor?
Have you left him some food?
Will you buy me a cell-phone?

Advice
Work hard that you may pass.
Work hard so that you may pass. (Meaning same as above)
Work hard lest you should not fail. (Meaning same as above - Lest takes should)

Habit (Similar sentences)
1. Subject + like to + verb
He likes to beg.
2. Subject + like to + gerund
He likes begging.
3. Subject + has/have + the habit of + V^4 (ing)
He has the habit of begging.
4. Subject + is/am/are + in the habit of + V^4 (ing)
He is in the habit of begging.
5. Subject + is/am/are + used to + gerund
He is used to begging.
6. Subject + is/am/are + accustomed to + gerund
He is accustomed to begging.

Variation:-
She keeps murmuring.
She is always murmuring. (Meaning same)
She is constantly murmuring. (Meaning same)

He didn't write a letter nor will he.
You didn't buy a car nor can you.
He is not a leader not will he be.

He works hard with a view to success.
He went to London with a view to seeing his relatives.
He aims at success.
He wanders about aimlessly.
He is kicking the ball at random.
Is it any use to you?

Lesson 37

Wish (Similar sentences)
May he be successful!
I wish him success. (No article)
I wish that he get success. (Wrong sentence)
I wish him to get success.

I wish him write a book. (Desire)
I wish that he should write a book.
I will have him write a book. (Meaning – I wish him)
I would have him write a book. (Meaning – I wish him)
I want him to write a book.

Use of by
I went there by car. (Not, by a car)
I went there in a car. (In is used with article 'a' if the source is emphasized)
He travelled by road.
He earns by composing songs.
She maintains herself by coaching children.
I save money by not smoking.

Cause and Result (Similar sentences)
1. Principle clause + that + clause
He is so rich that he can buy a new car.
2. Principle clause + that + clause
So rich is he that he can buy a new car.
3. Subject + verb + adjective/adverb + enough + infinitive
He is rich enough to buy a new car.
4. It is + because + clause + so + clause
 It is because he is rich so he can buy a new car.

Contrast (Similar sentences)
Speak what you will, I can't agree with you.
Whatever you may speak, I can't agree with you.
Come what may, I can't agree with you.
Do as you will, I can't agree with you.

In spite of wealth, he is unhappy.
Despite wealth, he is unhappy.
For all his wealth, he is unhappy.

While she hates orphans, I love them.
Whereas she hates orphans, I love them. (Meaning same as above)
While on the one hand she hates orphans, I love them on the other. (Meaning same as above)

Lesson 38

Reason (Similar sentences)
As we are free, we can go out. | Since we are free, we can go out.
Seeing that we are free, we can go out. | Considering that we are free, we can go out.
Now that we are free, we can go out.

We can't go out in view of bad weather.
We can't go out on account of bad weather.
We can't go out owing to bad weather.

He got a job through his friend. (Though = because of)
You will get success through hard work.
Thanks to your help, I got this job.
I got this job but small thanks to you. (Meaning – I got the job not because of you)
He was fined for telling lies.
She couldn't speak anything for laughing.

Compound sentences
1. Partly because of + noun + and + partly because of + noun + sentence
Partly because of hunger and partly because of weakness he can't run.
2. What with + noun + and + what with + noun + sentence
What with hunger and what with weakness he can't run. (Meaning same as above)
3. Partly on account of + noun + and + partly on account of + noun + sentence
Partly on account of hunger and partly on account of weakness he can't run.
4. Partly owing to + noun + and + partly owing to + noun + sentence
Partly owing to hunger and partly owing to weakness he can't run.

How kind of you to help me! (Meaning – You helped me with kindness)
How clever of you to cheat him! (Meaning – You cheated him with cleverness)
Such a man and my husband! (Meaning – He can't be my husband)
To think of winning a lottery! (Meaning – It'll be a surprise if we win a lottery)

David sings and so does Martin.
The mother is beautiful and so is the daughter.
David doesn't sing and Martin doesn't sing either.
The mother isn't beautiful and the daughter isn't beautiful either.
David doesn't sing and neither does Martin.
The mother isn't beautiful and neither is the daughter.

Variation:-
If you work hard, you will be successful. (Not, will work hard)
If you work hard, <u>then</u> you will be successful. (Emphatic)
Unless you work hard, you can't be successful. (Condition)
Until you work hard, you can't be successful. (Time)
Do you want to be successful? Then work hard.

Lesson 39

Question tag
He is rich, isn't he?
He is rich, I believe. (Meaning same as above)
She can help you, can't she?
She can help you, I hope. (Meaning same as above)

Interrogative
What does he write? (Not, what he writes?)
When did he play? (Not, when he played?)
I know when he played. (Not, when did he play – because first clause is affirmative)
Do you know where he lives? (Not, where does he live)
Whom/who do you want to meet? (Whom, who – both are correct)
You cannot do this work. (Not, can not)
Isn't he playing? (Not, is he not)
Aren't they singing? (Not, are they not)

Comparative
1. The comparative + clause + the + comparative + clause
The higher we go, the colder it is.
The sooner you begin the work, the better it is.
2. Subject + get/grow + comparative + and + comparative
The patient is getting worse and worse.
The student is getting better and better.

State
Spring is come. (Not, has come – with underlined verbs only is/are is used)
He is gone to Mumbai.
The snow is melted.
My bag is lost.
The tree is fallen.
He became a minister.
He went mad.
Mangoes turned red.
The telephone went dead.
It is getting dark.
The college is in session.
The negotiation is in progress.
The election is in full swing.
He is on/off duty.

I saw her sing. (Meaning – I saw singing from beginning till end)
I saw her singing. (I saw while she was singing – didn't see end)
I saw the thief running away. (Incomplete state – work was not done)
I saw the thief run away. (Complete state – work was done)
I saw the thief to run away. (Wrong sentence)

Lesson 40

Emphatic with New rules (Similar sentences)
1. As + subordinate clause + principle clause
As I left home, it began to rain.
2. Just as + subordinate clause + principle clause
Just as I left home, it began to rain.
3. No sooner + helping verb + subordinate clause + principle clause
No sooner did I leave home <u>than</u> it began to rain.
4. As soon as + subordinate clause + principle clause
As soon as I left home, it began to rain.
5. Hardly/scarcely + had + clause + when/before + clause
Hardly had I left home when it began to rain.
Scarcely had I left home when it began to rain.

1. Not to speak of + noun/gerund + sentence
Not to speak of a coat, he doesn't have even a shirt. (Don't use - ~~what to speak/say of~~)
2. Let alone + noun/gerund + sentence
Let alone a coat, he doesn't have even a shirt. (Meaning same as above)
3. Sentence + much less + additional
He doesn't have even a shirt, much less a coat. (Meaning same as above)

<u>Emphatic Negative</u>
1. Neither + negative sentence + nor + helping verb + noun/pronoun
Neither I play nor does he.
2. Negative sentence + and + negative sentence + either
I don't play and he doesn't play either.
3. Negative sentence + and + neither + helping verb + noun/pronoun
I don't play and neither does he.
4. Negative sentence + nor + helping verb + subject
I don't play nor will I.

Not only he reads but also understands.
He not only reads but also understands. (Meaning same as above)
He not only reads. He understands as well. (Meaning same as above)

It is I who <u>has</u> written this book. (Not, have)
I myself <u>have</u> done this work. (Not, has)
He does know English. (Emphatic)
She did see me. (Emphatic)

He begins to laugh.
He starts laughing. (Meaning same as above)
He does nothing but laugh. (Meaning same as above)

All these lessons are the result of tremendous efforts of years. I am sure it gives you everything you were looking for in English. You must have to practice for it.

Miscellaneous
Here is a list of some more sentences that you can get yourself familiar with.

He lives in a place of a house. (Meaning – His house is like a place)
There are fewer women than children.
There are two persons less for work.
Smoking isn't as injurious as drinking.
Keeping a promise isn't as easy as making it.
He is stronger and more intelligent than his brother.
She is more brave than wise. (Not, wiser)
I shouldn't mind a cup of tea. (Meaning – I want to have tea)
This dress is her choice. (Not, of her choice)
It is I/me. (I or me – both are correct)
Do you want to ask anything?
Do you want to ask something? (Something can be used when you are in doubt)
He is continuously teaching.
He is continually teaching. (Giving a break)
He also helped me.
He, too, helped me. (Used with comma)
I help even enemies, much more friends.
Now he laughs now he cries.
This gate closes of itself.
Go to dogs! (Meaning – Go to hell)
Par excellence it is! (Meaning – How good it is!)

His absence was due to illness.
He was absent due to illness. (Before 'due to' noun comes, not adjective)
He has a house to live in.
We have hands to work with.
Note it down lest you should not forget it.
Note it down so that you may not forget it.
She pushed the door open. (Not, to open)
The murderer who was found guilty was hanged. (No comma)
I have as many pens as he. (Don't use – he has)
This is the same pen as Mark's. (Not, as of)
Whether teachers or students, all were present.
Whether oil or butter, everything is dear.
He not only reads but also understands.
Not only he reads but also understands. (Not only comes after subject)
He not reads. He understands as well.
He didn't harm, rather, he helped me.
He didn't harm me. On the contrary, he helped me.
Village after village was burnt down.
Sorrow after sorrow continued.
Day after day rolled on.
It is they who have abused him. (Not, them)

I <u>want</u> to ask you something. (Strong expression)
I <u>wanted</u> to ask you something. (Politeness)
I was wandering if you can answer my question. (Circumlocution)
What's on at Delhi? (Program)
She laughed her thanks. (She thanked with laugh)
She smiled her thanks.

Now as you have learnt all this, spend time for English and start taking the tasks where you can use this knowledge. Remember, you have to use your knowledge if you want to save it from being washed away.

Niranjan Jha Showman
www.facebook.com/cromosys
Nallasopara (W), Mumbai, India
+91-9561450045
cromosys@yahoo.com

Communicate with People

Listen to Them Carefully

Engage in Conversation

Develop Your Style

Read As Much As Possible

Speak Confidently

NIRANJAN JHA SHOWMAN

Founder - Niranjan Jha Showman

Education and Technology Research Center

Patankar Park, Nallasopara (W), Mumbai. +91-9561450045

Education, Technology, Publication, Healthcare, Newsmedia, Realtor, Filmmaking

www.facebook.com/cromosys

Cromosys Publication
Teach
Yourself
German
NIRANJAN JHA SHOWMAN

Cromosys Publication
Teach
Yourself
French
NIRANJAN JHA SHOWMAN

Cromosys Publication
Teach
Yourself
Spanish
NIRANJAN JHA SHOWMAN

Cromosys Publication

English
Voice
Accent and
Pronunciation

NIRANJAN JHA SHOWMAN

Teach Yourself Autodesk MAYA

Cromosys Publication

NIRANJAN JHA SHOWMAN

Cromosys Publication
Teach
Yourself
Autodesk
3ds Max
NIRANJAN JHA SHOWMAN

Cromosys Publication
CRIMINAL FACTORY
NIRANJAN JHA SHOWMAN

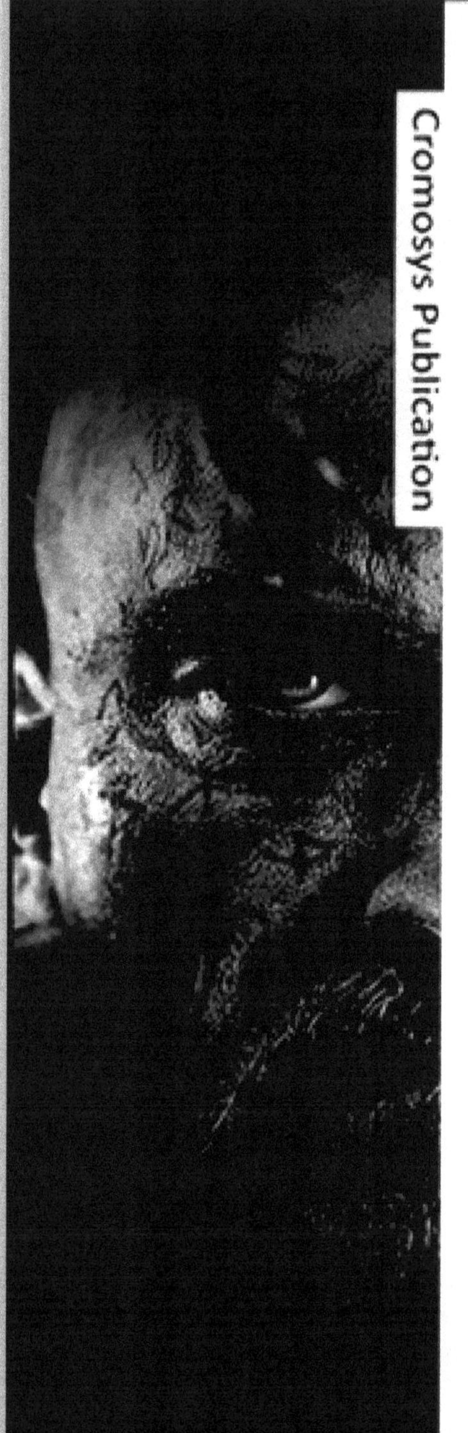

Cromosys Publication

FOCAL DISASTER

NIRANJAN JHA SHOWMAN

Cromosys Publication
Your talents will not help you succeed without your skill of using them.
NIRANJAN JHA SHOWMAN
BE
MILLIONAIRE
LIKE
ME

Copyright Office
Government of India

सत्यमेव जयते

Extracts
from the Register
of Copyrights

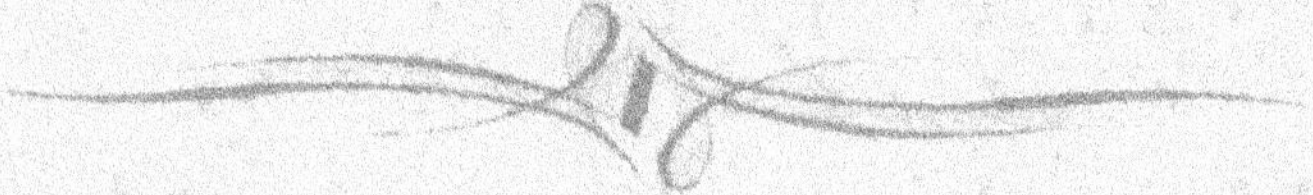

Dated : 17/08/2022

1.	Registration Number	:	**T-98713-2022**
2.	Name, address and nationality of the applicant	:	NIRANJAN JHA SHOWMAN, CROMOSYS PUBLICATION, 001, JAYSATYAM, PATANKAR ROAD, NALLASOPARA (W), MUMBAI, MAHARASHTRA - 401203. INDIAN
3.	Nature of the applicant's interest in the copyright of the work	:	AUTHOR
4.	Class and description of the work	:	LITERARY / BOOK
5.	Title of the work	:	**Dynamic Grammar of English**
6.	Language of the work	:	ENGLISH
7.	Name, address and nationality of the author and if the author is deceased, date of his decease	:	NIRANJAN JHA SHOWMAN, CROMOSYS PUBLICATION, 001, JAYSATYAM, PATANKAR ROAD, NALLASOPARA (W), MUMBAI, MAHARASHTRA - 401203. INDIAN
8.	Whether the work is published or unpublished	:	UNPUBLISHED
9.	Year and country of first publication and name, address and nationality of the publisher	:	N.A.
10.	Years and countries of subsequent publications, if any, and names, addresses and nationalities of the publishers	:	N.A. SAME AS ABOVE
11.	Names, addresses and nationalities of the owners of various rights comprising the copyright in the work and the extent of rights held by each, together with particulars of assignments and licences, if any	:	
12.	Names, addresses and nationalities of other persons, if any, authorised to assign or licence of rights comprising the copyright	:	N.A.
13.	If the work is an 'Artistic work', the location of the original work, including name, address and nationality of the person in possession of the work. (In the case of an architectural work, the year of completion of the work should also be shown).	:	N.A.
14.	If the work is an 'Artistic work', whether it is registered under the Designs Act 2000 if yes give details.	:	N.A.
15.	If the work is an 'Artistic work', capable of being registered as a design under the Designs Act 2000.whether it has been applied to an article though an industrial process and ,if yes ,the number of times it is reproduced.	:	N.A.
16.	Remarks, if any	:	

Diary Number :	9766/2020-DF/T
Date of Application :	25/07/2021
Date of Receipt :	25/07/2021

DEPUTY REGISTRAR OF COPYRIGHTS

www.ingramcontent.com/pod-product-compliance
Lightning Source LLC
Chambersburg PA
CBHW040909130726

48005CB00019BA/3033